I0004979

Book 1
Open Source
By Solis Tech

&

Book 2
Quality Assurance
By Solis Tech

Book 1
Open Source

By Solis Tech

Understanding Open Source From the Beginning!

Open Source: Understanding Open Source From the Beginning!

© Copyright 2015 – Solis Tech All rights reserved.

In no way is it legal to reproduce, duplicate, or transmit any part of this document in either electronic means or in printed format. Recording of this publication is strictly prohibited and any storage of this document is not allowed unless with written permission from the publisher. All rights reserved.

Table Of Contents

Introduction...26

Chapter 1: The Basics of Open Source...27

Chapter 2: History, Comparisons, and Relevance..............................30

Chapter 3: The Benefits and the Downsides of Open Source.............34

Chapter 4: The Open Source Culture...37

Chapter 5: The Future of Open Source...40
Conclusion...4

Introduction

I want to thank you and congratulate you for purchasing the book, *"Open Source: Understanding Open Source From the Beginning!"*

This book contains the basics in understanding the open source concept. What is it all about? Where did it come from? Who creates the open source content? How can software be considered as an 'open source'? What makes it different from the other software that we already have?

These questions are answered in this book. Also included in this book are information relevant to open source, such as examples of licensing, the Four Freedoms of free software use, and ideas about software piracy. This information will help to further understand what it means to have some software that is open sourced.

Real life comparisons are also made in this book in case you become confused or lost in understanding the open source concept. The idea of open source seems very simple, but in reality, it is very complex, with definitions coinciding with the definitions of other concepts such as free software (which will further be discussed in Chapter Two). Listed down in the book are the advantages and disadvantages of open source software, and the reasons why more and more people are becoming enticed with the idea of converting to open source.

If the present generation already dictates the movement of open source software, what will become of it in the future? This question is also answered in the last chapter of this book. Due to the fast-paced advancement of technology, open source will adapt to this advancement with the help of both developers and users.

Thanks again for purchasing this book, I hope you enjoy it!

Chapter 1: The Basics of Open Source

Have you ever wondered how an application you're using works? Every time you use an application and it freezes, do you think about what could have gone wrong? Do you ever think of why applications are constantly updating? These are questions that you would not be asked often. But these questions are very important to you, as a user of the Internet age.

Application programs are comprised of source codes, and these source codes are made by programmers. These codes are what allow you to type words into a word processing document, or to click on that video of cats meowing simultaneously. What you see onscreen are only visual representations of the codes of the program. Your application programs may be paid, or pre-installed in your devices, so you don't have permission to view these codes. Rather, you get the pre-made product, and you as a consumer have no power over it except to use it as instructed.

When you purchase or download an application and place it in your device, it installs a lot of files, but none of these files contain the source code. A software manager is included in your installed files to monitor the application as you use it. Whenever your application gets bugged or freezes, this software manager runs, and it prompts you to file a report to the software's developers to tell them exactly what happened. Once the report is filed, the developers study the bug, fix it, and release an update a few days or weeks later.

But what if you could see these codes for yourself? What if, whenever something goes wrong with the application, you could easily contact the developers or ask for help from other programmers easily? These questions are the foundations of open source, and you are about to learn more about it in the following chapters.

What is Open Source?

Open source is a computer program that has its source code visible to the public. The public – which we can refer to as the users – have the power to view, copy, and modify the source codes to their liking. The source code and the compiled version of the code are distributed freely to the users without fixed fees. Users of open source can pretty much do anything they like with the open source programs that they downloaded, since there are practically no restrictions.

To better understand the concept of open source software, let us use an example of recipes for comparison.

Recipes start off with someone writing them down on a piece of paper. A grandma, perhaps, has a recipe for a cake, which she writes in her recipe book. She passes on this recipe to her children, and tells them that they can use the recipe whenever they like. But, they must make sure to credit her as the original creator of the recipe.

The children recreate the recipe and whenever they are asked where the recipe is from, they would always tell that it's from grandma. One of grandma's children alters the cake recipe by adding strawberries as an extra ingredient. The grandma allows this, given that she is also permitted to use the altered recipe.

This example has the same concept with open source software.

When a programmer writes a code, compiles it into a program, and distributes both the source code and the compiled program to the users, he is giving everyone permission to access everything about the program. Users can run the program, view the code, modify if needed, compile, and redistribute the modified version of the program.

The original programmer, however, would require the users to let him use the modified versions of his program, since it is his to begin with. Aside from this certain restriction, the users of the program have the freedom to do whatever they like to do with it.

Let's go back to the example of the cake recipe. One of grandma's children, the one who added the strawberries, suggests to grandma to add the strawberries to the original recipe. The grandma thinks that this is a good idea therefore she complies and replaces her old recipe with the altered cake recipe.

In open source software, if the programmer is notified of a certain modification of a user, and it is deemed to be a modification that the software needs, then the programmer will revise his program based on that certain modification. This modification is called a patch. The user who has suggested of the modification is now coined as a contributor. This process of adapting user modification to an open source software is called upstreaming, because the modification goes back to the original code.

The concept of open source depends on the communication and collaboration between the software's developers and its users. Bug detection and fixing of open source is made easier because numerous users are working simultaneously to study the source code and to compile a modified, fixed version of the code.

With open source, it is not only the developers who are finding new ways on how the software can be improved and upgraded. The users can also contribute their ideas and knowledge in the upgrading of the software. The original developer or programmer can be called the maintainer who monitors the changes in his or her original software.

Let us then go back to the cake recipe. What if another child of grandma decides to do his own version of the cake recipe? He adds raisins to the cake recipe, and asks grandma if the raisins can be added with the strawberries in the original recipe. Grandma refuses, because she dislikes raisins. Instead of being disheartened, this child decides that he would create his own version of the recipe and share it with the people he knows.

If a certain modification makes no appeal to the developer, the one who suggested the modification may opt to make his own version of the program. This act of not patching a modification from the original program is called forking. A forked program is a certain program that alters the original program in such a way that it becomes its own program.

A forked program can be described as a chip off an old block, since it doesn't necessarily separate itself from the license of the program it originated from, although it may seem like it due to the avoidance of patching. Programmers that collaborate with open source result to forking if their modified versions of the original program are deemed unfit by the program's developer.

Nonprofit organizations are the prime developers of open source software. However, due to the freedom of customization that open source has given both users and developers, even large companies are adhering to the open source culture.

How did Open Source become popular?

During the early times of computing, software followed a protocol and design with everyone conforming to a certain cookie-cutter ideal. Software was yet to be imagined as cost-free, and the developers kept their codes to themselves. But then, during the early 90's, the idea of sharing one's code to the public became an accepted idea to most users. The concept of software being free and open sourced became a reality when, after decades, the likes of Mozilla Firefox and OpenOffice were created.

Open source rose in its ranks when developers started making open source alternatives of commercial software. These alternatives are free and can easily be downloaded from the internet, enticing most users to convert to open source. What made open source rise, however, was the idea of community. Fellow programmers could interact and communicate with each other, and even with the developers, which was unheard of during the early times of computing. People could collaborate with the developers of the software and share their insights.

Open source has also given its users the freedom to fully inspect software before they use it – an action that was impossible to do with closed source software. Users who are into coding try open source and study the code line by line.

The popularity of open source software has been anticipated due to the fact that a lot of people supported the cause. Programmers started creating open source projects to contribute to the cause, and users started to get accustomed to obtaining and downloading open source software. With volunteers signing up left and right, and organizations creating their own programs, the growth and expansion of open source software cannot be stopped anymore.

Chapter 2: History, Comparisons, and Relevance

Open source was not immediately implemented until the early 90's, where more and more people began to realize the importance of being able to share the source code of software without fees and royalties. Like any other idea, open source started out as a small thought of making software free for the public, and grew into the culture that it is today.

The History of Open Source: The Open Source Initiative

Eric Raymond, an American software developer, published an essay (turned book) entitled The Cathedral and the Bazaar in 1997. The essay speaks about two different types of software, which he labels the Cathedral and the Bazaar.

In the essay, Raymond describes the Cathedral to be the type of software in which with each release of software, the source code of the software will be available. However, with each build of the software, the certain code block that has been modified is restricted to only the developers of the software. The examples presented under the Cathedral type of software were GNU Emacs (a type of text editor) and the GNU Compiler Collection (a compiler that caters to different programming languages).

In contrast, the Bazaar is the type of software that has the Internet as the venue for their development, making the code visible to the public. The example presented under the Bazaar type of software was Linux (now a widely known computer operating system), in which Raymond coined the developer Linus Torvalds to be the creator of the Bazaar type of software.

Raymond's article became popular in 1998, getting the attention of major companies and fellow programmers. Netscape was influenced by this article, leading them to release the source codes of their internet suite called Netscape Communicator. The source code of the said internet suit was what gave birth to internet browsers such as Thunderbird and SeaMonkey. Mozilla Firefox, a popular web browser today, was also based from the source codes of Netscape Communicator.

The idea of source codes being free became widespread when Linux was developed, urging people to contribute to the open source cause. Because of the increasing popularity of Linux and similar projects, people who became interested in the cause formed the Open Source Initiative, a group whose advocacy is to tell people about the benefits of open sourcing and why it is needed in the computing world.

Open Source vs. Free Software

Most people confused open source software with free software, as the two terms share somewhat the same advocacy. With understanding, it is not that difficult to tell these two terms apart.

The difference between free software and open source software can be listed down into different points. Although they have their differences, both free software and open source software have a singular goal – to publicize source codes for the users to see.

Free software focuses mainly on the ethical aspect of the advocacy. There are certain freedoms that free software are fighting for when it comes to the use of software, which cannot be given to the users by commercial software. These are the Four Freedoms of software use according to advocates of free software:

- The freedom to use the software. This means that the user is free to use the software to his or her needs, or as instructed.

- The freedom to study the source codes of the software. Since the codes are readily available for public viewing, the user has the freedom to view and study the said codes. After he or she reviews the codes, he or she then has the freedom to do the next step.

- The freedom to modify the source codes of the software to the user's liking. If necessary, the user has the freedom to customize the source code and to create a version of the program fit for the user's specific needs.

- The freedom to share the modified, compiled source codes to the public. If the program has been modified, the user has the freedom to compile and publish the modified program for the benefit of the other users who may also have the need of the program's modification. The developer of the original program should also be given the freedom and right to use the modified version of the program.

Free software allows its users to do whatever they want with a program. If they want to modify the source code and redistribute the modified code as their own, without the consent of the original developers, then they are free to do so. If the user wishes to use the source code as the base code of a new project that they are working on, then they will not be sued. The ethical reasoning of free software simply states that there are no grave restrictions when it comes to copying, revising, and republishing the already existing software.

Open source, on the other hand, creates programs with the Four Freedoms in mind. The programs which are considered open source are made for the user's convenience and benefit. The common idea of open source is a group of people working on a single open source project, attempting to create a program that will be beneficial to them, as well as the users.

Open Source and Paid Software

Open source software did indeed come from paid software. There are countless of open source alternatives for common, commercially-sold software readily available on the internet. Some examples of this are office suites like LibreOffice and OpenOffice, which are open source alternatives for the much more popular Microsoft Office.

The reason why open source alternatives of paid software exist is mainly the cost. Users would opt to pay less, or none at all, for certain software. Why pay for software when there are free alternatives that can be downloaded from the internet easily? Open source makes it possible for users who cannot afford paid software to experience the basic and intermediate features of the software, without sacrificing the quality of the end product.

Although open source may be the overall solution for users to get a feel of certain software, there are still others who would want to obtain paid software but through illegal means. This is called software piracy, an action that is still evident despite it being illegal in most countries.

Software piracy is the act of downloading or installing a paid software illegally, either through software cracks or illegally burned CDs. The most popular way to obtain pirated software is through downloading Torrent-based software crack, in which the user can get the files through different computers almost discreetly. Since these software are pirated, installing these software requires the user to turn off his or her Internet connection before installing, to avoid being tracked.

Some paid software can be bought once, and shared with different computers or devices. All of the information regarding the sharing of paid software can be found on the software's End User License Agreement or EULA. The EULA is a splash screen shown at the start of the software's installation which contains the contract between the software's developers and the user.

The EULA may allow the user to share one copy of the software to different devices, or it may restrict the user from doing so. Once the user has violated this part of the EULA, it can then be considered as software piracy.

Something that a user should be aware of is a certain license called the GNU General Public License, the license that most open source software adhere to. The license permits the user to copy, modify, and redistribute the modified code, just as long as the source files and the original codes are still documented. This is important in understanding how and why open source software is allowed to move freely across the internet without being coined as software piracy, as compared to paid, propriety software.

With propriety or paid software, the user is buying only the license. He is not allowed to revise the code, to reverse-engineer the code, and to view the code by all means. The only thing that the user is allowed to do when he purchases propriety software is to use a copy of the software that the developer has provided. It may seem like an unfair deal to some people, because a user should be able to own something that he has paid for.

Open source software changes that idea. It gives the user the freedom to see the program's source code, letting the user know the program's 'skeletal system'. Even without paying for the software, the user gets the full potential functions of the software and not just an executable copy of it.

Importance of Open Source

Technology is rapidly changing. Experts are coming up with more ways to improve the lives of other people. It is the same with those who contribute to open source projects. Their advocacy is to create free programs that will benefit the users.

Open source is important in the evolution of quality software. With a lot of people contributing to one singular project, the software that is produced will be the best of its kind as it has been meticulously observed and reviewed by the contributors. Open source gives way for the collaborative effort of different programmers and users, with the users being secondary developers of a certain program. It is an interactive effort, with the users being able to update the program alongside the developers themselves.

The fast paced advancement of technology would often overwhelm content creators to the point that they would stop creating content altogether. Content creators who are left behind by technology's advancement are often working in small groups or on their own, and have no means of help from fellow creators of their kind.

With Open source, this is never the case. Each open source software has its own community to back a fellow programmer up during each build, ready to help out other programmers and users when needed. The open source community's bond with each other is what makes open source catch up with the fast advancement of technology.

Chapter 3: The Benefits and the Downsides of Open Source

The Benefits of Open Source

The most obvious perk of having open source software is the availability of the source code. With the source code available to the general public, people are able to study the code line by line. Students of programming can study the source code and implement some blocks of it into their own projects, honing their skills and improving their code. Users who are meticulous with their software can view the codes and customize the said codes to their liking.

Aside from the source codes being publicized, another perk of having open source software is that it is mostly free, depending on the software's license. Users of open source software do not have to pay a large sum of money to be able to enjoy the full functions of the software. If the license requires the user to pay, the user may still try out the software's full functions before purchasing.

Open source promotes community. If a user encounters a problem with the downloaded software, he or she can seek help from fellow programmers or the developers themselves through a forum. Users and programmers alike can communicate and share their experiences with using the software, helping other users to get used to the software. With other programmers keen on editing and revising the source code, updated and better versions of the software can easily be uploaded and shared within the community for the benefit of the other users.

Also, when something goes wrong with the open source software, the user has the option to fix the problem himself should seeking help be an option that is not convenient for him. In propriety software, this cannot be possible as the license and copyright prohibits its users from ever touching the program's source code.

If the user of propriety software does as much as reverse-engineer the product, then they could be violating the program's copyright and therefore, be taken to jail. Open source software removes this restriction from the users, giving them permission to fix solvable program problems on their own.

The benefits of open source software are not limited to personal use. Companies and businesses are adhering to the open source paradigm due to the endless possibilities at half the price or lesser.

More and more businesses are converting to open source mainly because it is more cost-efficient than purchasing commercial software. Companies also have more freedom with open source software in terms of customization, since they have the power to mold the software to fit their company's needs. These factors are beneficial in the growth and development of businesses in such a way that the businesses need not to put out a large sum of money just to be able to acquire a software that will be utilized in their business.

Open sourcing has become a way for people to have access to the things that they initially did not have access to. Users of software now have the ability to study the source code of the program they are using, and to know how exactly a certain function of the program runs by looking at its specific line of code.

A sense of community is also created between the software's developers and programmers from outside of their firms. Through open sourcing, the developers are able to communicate with other programmers with regards to how the software can be enhanced further.

Some users would say that using open source operating systems grants more security as compared to paid operating systems. For example, if a user installs the Linux operating system, he or she does not need an antivirus or a virus detection software to keep his or her files intact. The operating system itself has security measures for the user. This becomes a benefit for both professional and nonprofessional users because they have more room for important files rather than installing different kinds of applications for protection.

Open source software is made for the people, by the people. It hones itself to the needs and wants of each user. Because of this, there is no need for the user to upgrade his or her hardware every time the software upgrades.

Take Apple's OSX (operating system) for example. Certain updates of the operating system are available to download, with better features than the previous build. However, older versions of the Macbook and the iMac cannot avail of the recent builds as their hardware are not fit enough to accommodate either the size of the downloaded file or the features itself.

With open source software, the upgrades can be coded to fit each user's needs, depending on the user's hardware. If a certain upstreamed version of the open source software is available to download, different downloaders are made available by the developer with the specifications listed beside each downloader, catering to the different specifications of the user. The user himself can opt to customize the code of the program to be compatible with his device.

Allowing the user these freedoms over the software has given open source software a bit of a leverage over paid, propriety software. But then again, there will be nay-sayers who think that open source software isn't the way to go.

The Downsides and Disadvantages of Open Source

Open sourcing has given users lots of benefits, but it is not perfect. Some would still prefer paid software over any open sourced software. Here are some of the reasons why some users do not approve of open source.

If a user is not in any way a technology expert, he or she would want software that is easy to use. Open source software is known to be more technical compared to their paid counterparts. Paid software focuses on its user interface, making the application easy for the user to understand the system. Open source software usually start out with a not so attractive user interface, but with the basic functions of the program intact. As the program gets updated with each build, the user interface changes and adapts to the needs of its users.

Most critics would say that paid or propriety software is still better in a number of factors as compared to open source software. Because more people are accustomed to using paid or propriety software, the idea that there are other types of software available is intimidating to them. People think that open source software is made only for the technology savvy users, with the interface hard for them to manipulate. Why download a complicated software when they can buy a simple, pre-made software that they are already familiar with?

Paid software has become a norm in the everyday lives of users. Large companies such as Microsoft and Apple have made their name known all throughout the world, creating technologies that users and consumers have grown to love. Because of their undying popularity, the rise of open source software is unknown to the general public. And even if they are known, those who are used to seeing the big names are hesitant to try out what open source might be.

Seeking technical help might seem simple with the numerous open source communities readily available, but it may sometimes be inconvenient to the user. Paid software offer professional tech support straight from the manufacturers.

Chapter 4: The Open Source Culture

Open source gives the user freedom to do whatever he or she wants in a software. Who wouldn't want the freedom to edit source codes to their own liking? With open source, this opportunity of customization is available at hand.

Why are more people converting to open source?

With the source code open for public scrutiny, looking for errors will be easier. Other software companies that do not have their source code publicized have their own set of programmers and developers figuring out the bugs in the software. This is an advantage for companies who always require their software to be updated regularly to keep up with the business.

Students who cannot afford the luxury of paid software turn to their open source counterparts to be able to utilize their functions without having to pay a large amount of money. Open source alternatives of Microsoft Office are available for the students to download should they need to use an office suite for their projects.

Some open source versions of paid software are actually better. Paid media players can play certain file types and extensions, but crash once the file extension is unrecognizable. Open source software developers take note of these bugs and create a media player that can play almost all media file types and extensions in high definition. Because of this, even users who are not actually technology savvy would convert to the open source alternatives of paid software just because they've heard and they know that they can get more out of the open source counterpart.

Programmers who want to practice their coding also rely on readily available open source software in their study. Because the codes of open source can easily be viewed and modified, programmers can base their project on open source software and publish it as their own, creating a program fork.

Businesses, on the other hand, turn to open source software for two main factors: cost efficiency and the power of customization. As mentioned in a previous chapter, with open source software readily available to download on the internet, the businesses do not need to spend a lot of money for a software that they cannot customize as their own. Open source gives them the opportunity to keep on upgrading their system as needed, therefore improving the quality of their software with each build.

The flexibility of open source software has enticed businesses to change to open source from propriety software. Businesses would often buy already existing software and attempt to use them as instructed by the developers. Open source software has its own rules and regulations, but if businesses want their software to be something specific, then the developers of open source software will deliver. With propriety software, the business is the one to adjust to the software that they have purchased, an action that is removed once businesses convert to open source.

Examples of Open Source Software

A wide variety of open source software are available for download. These software may be used for utility purposes, for multimedia purposes – anything that the user desires and requires. Here are a few examples of open source software that you as a user have probably heard of.

The prime example of open source software is an operating system called Linux. It is an operating system based off of UNIX that is available to different computer platforms and hardware.

Another example of open source software is the media player called VLC Media Player developed by the VideoLAN Organization. This media player can run a variety of multimedia files at high definition. Its paid counterpart is Microsoft's own Windows Media Player, which before its most recent build can only play a handful of file extensions.

When it comes to operating systems, Android is another popular example of open source software. A company called Android, Inc. (later bought by Google) has developed this mobile operating system using another open source kernel, Linux. It caters mostly to devices which have touchscreen on them, such as touchscreen desktop monitors, tablets, and smartphones, much like its counterpart from Apple called iOS. Android has its own application store called Google Play, where the users can install applications onto their phones mostly for free.

Netbeans, a well-known software developing application, is also an example of an open source software. It is a Java-created application that caters to different programming languages, and can be run on multiple operating systems. Programmers use Netbeans to create object oriented applications using the 24 programming languages that it caters to.

GIMP, or GNU Image Manipulation Program, is an Adobe Photoshop-like application that edits photos and creates graphic images. It has basic photo editing features such as cropping, grayscaling, and resizing, making it a simpler alternative to Photoshop. Like its paid counterpart, users of GIMP can also create animated GIF images, a feature that most multimedia artists are very fond of using.

Video and computer games can also be open sourced. Some open source games such as Tux Racer are available in the Linux package when downloaded. The principle of open source games is the same as any other open source software – the developers merging and collaborating with the users to create quality content to be distributed to the general public. However, the visual quality and elements of open source games are yet to be improved.

Other examples include PHP (a web development language), MySQL (used in databases alongside applications such as Microsoft Access and Microsoft Visual Basic), Python (programming language), Blender (an Autocad Maya-esque application that caters to 3D rendering), and many more.

Chapter 5: The Future of Open Source

What will happen in the future?

The future of open sourcing seems bright. With most businesses converting to open source software and most developers contributing to open source projects, the growth and expansion of open sourcing will continue. Open sourcing gives way for the innovation of modern software technology – with a lot of people working on one simple open source project, there is no doubt that the project will continue to be updated and improved.

Software will only continue to improve as time passes by. Open source software has made it easier for software to improve and upgrade itself due to countless of volunteers who are up to the challenge. While propriety software claim to start software trends, open source software advocates the upgrades of software that will be favorable to the needs of the users rather than to the bank accounts of the developers.

Open source software does not wish to waste the time and money of the user; rather, it aims to maximize both time and money, with the inclusion of effort, of the user when utilizing the software.

Presently, paid software are still dominant over open source software. Paid software have more leverage compared to open source software when it comes to reliability and familiarity, since they have been used by programmers and users alike for decades. There is still a certain percentage of users who are not aware that there are open source versions of their paid software, which they can help improve and customize to their own needs and liking.

More people will be aware of the benefits of open source software in the future. With propriety software releasing more licenses that restrict its users from certain software freedom, the existence of open source will lead to the users converting from propriety software due to the lack of free will.

In the future, there is a possibility that open source will be available not just for software, but also for other forms of content that have sources.

The future of open source as an idea or a paradigm will not be restricted to software alone. With the further advancement of technology, more and more gadgets will be locked down by licenses and warranties which restrict its users from fixing even simple problems that the product may have.

Gadgets are becoming more and more digitized, and copyright restricts people from ever touching or attempting to change the software. Because of this, some people are beginning to open up to the idea of open source not just for software, but also for hardware and gadgets that are used every day.

Let us take tractors for example. Tractors are machines that are essential in farming. If a tractor breaks down, the farmer himself can fix the broken tractor and keep it running again without having to buy a new one. But the modernization of technology leads the manufacturers of tractors to add digital aspects into their products: tractors now have microchips and are operated via computers, therefore are now protected by copyright.

Now, if the new tractor breaks down, the farmer has no permission to fix the tractor himself. He must hire a specialist to fix the problem, or else he goes to jail.

Open source hardware has already started to rise in its ranks alongside open source software. It basically means that users are free to create their gadgets from scratch, using open source hardware. Although the idea seems taboo at present, the fact that gadgets are also being restricted from the users will give way for both open source hardware and software to rise even further, giving users complete freedom over the creation and implementation of the technology that they need.

Content creators are restricted from creating certain things just because of copyright laws. Even artists, who upload videos on websites like YouTube and Vimeo, get flagged just because of a certain song or a certain speech that had some sort of copyright over it. This restricts creative freedom. It also restricts the content creators from creating what they know and love, and sharing it with their viewers.

Will open sourcing become a culture in the future? Surely, with the massive amounts of information available for the users to share freely amongst themselves. Open source software has given way for an idea that will change the world of computing for everyone, and allows everyone to have access to the large chunk of information that was previously not available to them. Transparency when it comes to creating code and building machines will become a fad in the future, as more and more people are willing and able to create content and share it with other users.

Conclusion

Thank you again for purchasing this book!

I hope this book was able to help you to understand better the concept of open source and its benefits to the public.

Finally, if you enjoyed this book, please take the time to share your thoughts and post a review on Amazon. It'd be greatly appreciated!

Thank you and good luck!

Book 2
Quality Assurance
By Solis Tech

Software Quality Assurance Made Easy!

Quality Assurance: Software Quality Assurance Made Easy!

© Copyright 2015 – Solis Tech All rights reserved.

In no way is it legal to reproduce, duplicate, or transmit any part of this document in either electronic means or in printed format. Recording of this publication is strictly prohibited and any storage of this document is not allowed unless with written permission from the publisher. All rights reserved.

.

Table Of Contents

Introduction......25

Chapter 1 Definition Of Software Quality Assurance And Software Testing......26

Chapter 2 Introducing Software Quality Assurance Procedures To An Existing Company......29

Chapter 3 Ensuring Software Quality......33

Chapter 4 How To Develop And Run Software Testing......36

Chapter 5 Deciding When To Release The Software To Users......39

Chapter 6 Using Automated Testing Tools......42

Conclusion......45

Introduction

I want to thank you and congratulate you for purchasing the book, *"Quality Assurance: Software Quality Assurance Made Easy"*.

This book contains proven steps and strategies on how to implement Software Quality Assurance.

Software quality assurance evolved from the quality assurance in industrial production in the 1940s. With the introduction of computers and the development of applications, it has become an important aspect of software development. In this book, you will learn about the various concepts of software quality assurance and its application in your workplace.

Chapter 1 talks about the definitions of software quality assurance and quality control. It is necessary that you understand what it is so that you can fully grasp the other fundamental concepts. Chapter 2 discusses the ways you can implement software quality assurance in an existing environment. In Chapter 3, you will learn how you can ensure that the software produces quality outputs.

Chapter 4 teaches you how to develop and run software testing while Chapter 5 talks about the timing of the software release. In Chapter 6, you will learn about using automated testing tools.

Thanks again for purchasing this book, I hope you enjoy it!

Chapter 1: Definition Of Software Quality Assurance And Software Testing

Software quality assurance is part of the process of software development. It includes the improvement and monitoring of the process. It also follows the processes, procedures, and standards. Furthermore, it ensures the resolution of problems discovered. In effect, it focuses on the prevention of problems.

Software testing, on the other hand, includes the operation of the application or system under controlled conditions, which must include all abnormal and normal conditions. The primary goal of software testing is to know what can go wrong when unexpected and expected scenarios occur. Its focus is on the detection of problems.

Companies differ in assigning responsibilities for quality assurance and software testing. There are organizations that combine both responsibilities to a single person or group. However, it is also common to have various teams that combine developers and testers. Project managers lead such teams. The decision to either combine or separate responsibilities depends on the company's business structure and size. Human beings or machines can perform software testing.

Some projects do not require a group of testers. The need for software testing depends on the project's context and size, the development methodology, the risks, the developers' experience and skill, and other factors. For example, a short-term, low-risk, and small project with expert developers, who know how to use test-first development or thorough unit testing, may not require software test engineers.

In addition, a small or new IT company may not have a dedicated software testing staff even its projects have a need for it. It may outsource software testing or use contractors. It may also adjust its approach on project development and management by using either agile test-first development or more experienced programmers. An inexperienced project manager may use his developers to do their own functional testing or skip thorough testing all together. This decision is highly risky and may cause the project to fail.

If the project is a huge one with non-trivial risks, software testing is important. The use of highly specialized software testers enhances the ability of the project to succeed because different people with different perspectives can offer their invaluable contribution because they have stronger and deeper skills.

In general, a software developer focuses on the technical issues to make a functionality work. On the other hand, a software test engineer focuses on what can go wrong with the functionality. It is very rare to come across a highly effective technical person, who can do both programming and testing tasks. As such, IT companies need software test engineers.

There are various reasons why software may have bugs. First, there is no communication or miscommunication as to the application's requirements. Second, the software is very complex so an inexperienced individual may have a difficult time understanding the software application. In addition, the software may be a big one and includes big databases, data communications, security complexities, different remote and local web services, and multi-tier distributed systems.

Third, there are programming errors. Fourth, the requirements of the software change because the end-user requests for them. In some cases, this end-user may not be aware of the effects of such changes, which can result in errors. The staff's enthusiasm is affected. Continuous modification requirements are a reality. Quality assurance and software test engineers must be able to plan and adapt continuous testing to prevent bugs from affecting the software.

Fifth, time pressures can be difficult to manage. Mistakes often occur during crunch times. Sixth, people involved in the project may not be able to manage their own egos. Seventh, the code has poor documentation or design. It is difficult to modify and maintain codes that are poorly written or documented. Bugs can occur if IT companies do not offer incentives for developers to write maintainable, understandable, and clear codes. Most companies offer incentives when they are able to finish the code quickly. Eighth, the use of software development tools can also result to bugs.

How Quality Assurance Evolved

In 1946, the US Occupation Forces established the Quality Movement in Japan. The movement follows the research of W. Edwards Deming and the Statistical Process Control papers. The methods discussed by the research and papers pertained to industrial production. Each process of production has an output with a required specification and a verifiable main product. The Quality Control group measures the output at different production stages. It ensures that the output falls within the acceptable variances.

The Quality Assurance group does not part in the production process. It audits the process to ensure compliance with the established standards and guidelines. It gives its input for the continuous improvement of the process. In a manufacturing setup, it is easy to differentiate between quality assurance and quality control. These methods become the norm in manufacturing. Since they work in industrial production, they spawned the birth of software quality control and software quality assurance.

Quality Attributes Of Software

Hewlett Packard's Robert Grady developed the common definition of the Software Quality Attributes. The FURPS model identified the following characteristics: functionality, usability, reliability, performance, and supportability (FURPS).

The functional attributes pertain to the features of the software. They answer the question about the purpose of the software instead of its use. The reason for the software's existence is different from the concerns about its reliability, look and feel, and security. The usability attributes are characteristics pertaining to user interface issues like consistency, interface aesthetics, and accessibility.

The reliability attributes include recoverability, accuracy, and availability of the system while performance attributes pertain to issues like startup time, recovery time, system response time, and information throughput. Supportability addresses issues like localizability, scalability, installation, configurability, compatibility, maintainability, adaptability, and testability. The FURPS model evolved into FURPS+ to include specification of constraints like physical, interface, implementation, and design constraints.

The Software Quality Control team tests the quality characteristics. The tests for usability and functionality occur during execution of the actual software. On the other hand, adaptability and supportability tests occur through code inspection. It is not the responsibility of the Software Quality Control or Software Quality Assurance to put the quality attributes into the software. The Software Quality Control team tests for the absence or presence of such characteristics while the Software Quality Assurance group ensures that each stakeholder follow the right standards and procedures during software execution.

In theory, the implementation of FURPS+ will overcome the problems caused by the software's intangible nature because the Software Quality Control team can measure each software attribute. For example, the amount of time it takes for programmers to fix a bug is a measure of supportability. To improve it requires the implementation of new coding standards.

The Software Quality Control group can inspect the code to ensure compliance with the coding standard while the Software Quality Assurance team can ensure that the quality control and programmer teams follow the right standards and process. It is the duty of the Software Quality Assurance group to collect and analyze the time spent on fixing the bug so that it can provide an input in terms of its usefulness to the process improvement initiative.

Chapter 2: Introducing Software Quality Assurance Procedures To An Existing Company

The introduction of the software quality assurance procedures rely on the risks involved and the company's size. If the organization is large and the projects are high-risk, the management must consider a more formal quality assurance process. On the other hand, if the risk is lower, the implementation of quality assurance may be a step-at-a-time procedure. The processes of quality assurance maintain balance with productivity.

If the project or the company is small, an ad-hoc process may be more appropriate. The success of the software development relies on the team leaders and developers. More importantly, there must be enough communications between software testers, managers, customers, and developers. Requirement specifications must be complete, testable, and clear. There must be procedures for design and code reviews, as well as retrospectives. Common approaches used are Agile, Kaizen, and Deming-Shewhart Plan-Do-Check-Act methods.

It is important to evaluate documents, code, specifications, plans, and requirements. To do this, it is necessary to prepare issues lists, checklists, inspection meetings, and walkthroughs. This process is what IT people refer to as verification. On the other hand, validation occurs after verification and includes actual testing of the application. A walkthrough is evaluation in an informal meeting. There is no need to prepare for it.

An inspection is more formal than a walkthrough and attended by at most eight people including a reader, a recorder, and a moderator. Usually, an inspection's subject is a test plan or requirements specification so that the attendees will know the software's problems. The attendees must read the document before attending an inspection so they will find the problems prior to the meeting. It is difficult to prepare for an inspection but it is an effective and least costly way to ensure quality.

Testing Requirements That Must Be Considered

The basis of black box testing is the software's functionality and requirements. A software tester need not be knowledgeable of code or internal design. White box testing, on the other hand, requires knowledge of code. It takes into consideration the code statements, paths, branches, and conditions. Unit testing requires testing of particular code modules or functions. Usually, the application developer performs it because it requires detailed knowledge of the code and program design.

API testing is testing of data exchange or messaging among systems parts. An incremental integration testing tests the application when there is a new functionality, which must be independent to work separately before it can be included in the application. The application programmer or software tester performs this type of testing. An integration testing requires the testing of the various parts of the software in order to know if they work together properly. Functional testing, on the other hand, is a kind of black box testing that focuses on the application's functional requirements. The software testers perform it.

System testing is also another type of black box testing. It includes testing of the general requirements specifications and all the various parts of the software. End-to-end testing, on the other hand, is a macro type of system testing. It includes testing the whole software in various situations that replicates real-world use. Smoke testing or sanity testing is an initial testing to know if the new version is performing well so that major testing can commence. Regression testing retests the application after some modifications or fixes.

Acceptance testing is final testing the software based on customer's specifications. Load testing is software testing under heavy loads in order to find out when the response time of the system fails or degrades. Stress testing, on the other hand, is system functional testing with unusually heavy loads, large complex queries of the database, using large numerical values, and heavy repetition of certain inputs or actions. Performance testing is testing using test or quality assurance plans.

The goal of usability testing depends on the customer or end-user. It uses techniques like surveys, user interviews, and user sessions' video recording. Software testers and developers are not the people to implement usability testing. Install/uninstall testing uses processes to test upgrade, full, or partial install/uninstall of the software. Recovery testing determines how the software can recover in catastrophic instances like hardware failures and crashes. Failover testing is another name for recovery testing.

Security testing tests how the application protects against willful damage, unauthorized access, and the likes. It uses sophisticated testing methods. Compatibility testing tests how the application performs in some environments. Exploratory testing, on the other hand, is an informal and creative testing that does not use any formal test cases or plans. Usually, software testers are new to the application. Ad-hoc testing is almost the same as exploratory testing but the software testers understand the application prior to testing.

Context-driven testing focuses on the software's intended use, culture, and environment. For example, medical equipment software has a different testing approach than a computer game. User acceptance testing determines if the application is satisfactory to the customer or end-user. Comparison testing, on the other hand, compares the software with its competitors.

Alpha testing occurs when the software is almost finished. Usually, end users perform this type of testing. Beta testing is testing when the software is finished and ready for final release. Like alpha testing, this kind of testing is for end users. Finally, mutation testing uses test cases and allows for code changes and retesting using the original test cases to discover software bugs.

Common Problems And Solutions In Developing Software

Software development can encounter common problems like poor user stories or requirements, unrealistic schedule, inadequate testing, featuritis, and miscommunication. Problems can arise if there requirements are incomplete, unclear, not testable, or too general. Furthermore, if the software development has a short timetable, problems can also be evident. If the software does not pass through the testing process, the IT organization will only know of problems if the system crashes or the end users complain.

In addition, problems can arise if the users or customers request for more new functionalities even after the development goals are set. Finally, if there is miscommunication between the programmers and customers, problems are inevitable. If it is an agile project, the problems become evident when it strays away from agile principles.

If there are common problem then there are also common solutions like solid requirements, realistic schedules, adequate testing, sticking to original requirements, and communication. Software requirements must be complete, clear, cohesive, detailed, testable, and attainable. All players concerned must agree upon them. In agile environments, there must be close coordination with end users or customers so that any change in requirement is clear. There must be enough time for design, planning, bug fixing, testing, changes, retesting, and documentation. Each person must not feel burnout during the project.

For testing to be adequate, it must start early. Retesting must occur after each change or fix. There must be enough time for bug fixing and testing. If the end user or customer requests for excessive changes when development has begun, it is important that the project manager explain the consequences. If the change is important, a schedule change is inevitable to accommodate it.

The project manager must manage the expectations of the end users or customer. In an agile environment, the project manager can expect significant change in the initial requirements. There must be a schedule for inspections and walkthroughs. The use of communication tools is important to ensure cooperation and teamwork.

Software Quality Assurance And Software Quality Control In The Workplace

If there is no formal implementation of Software Quality Assurance/Software Quality Control, the quality group can mirror that of an engineering services group. It performs the tasks not done by the development team. It reports to the application development manager. Under this scenario, the manager can instruct the quality assurance personnel to install a load-testing tool and declare him as a performance expert. Although the quality assurance person must perform load testing, it is the job of the software designer/programmer. As such, the software quality assurance/software quality control must be separate from the development team.

Software quality assurance requires the establishment of templates used during reviews. Such templates must have sections for both non-functional and functional requirements. For example, the requirements for performance must be in terms of transaction rates and user population. The use of Traceability Matrix can help in the requirements management. The matrix also encourages the analyst to use individual requirements for cross-referencing.

Software quality assurance verifies that the requirements comply with the templates and that they are not ambiguous. It reviews the risks of non-completion of the non-functional attributes, as well as the Traceability Matrix, to ensure usability of all requirements in other specifications. Software quality assurance can write the test cases, which refer to some of the requirements. It can cross-reference the requirements in the Traceability Matrix.

The interface specification is a requirement if the software is component-based. Software quality assurance must subject the document to verification. It must also subject other lower level specifications to quality assurance if such requirements are critical. Even if there are limited resources for software quality assurance, an IT organization can obtain a good return-on-investment if it pays attention to requirements and interfaces.

Chapter 3: Ensuring Software Quality

Software quality is the delivery of bug-free software within budget and on time. Because quality is subjective, it depends on the customer and his overall influence in the project. A customer can be an end user, a customer contract officer, a customer acceptance tester, a customer manager, a software maintenance engineer, and others. Each customer has his own definition of quality.

A code is good if it works, is secure, bug free, maintainable, and readable. Some companies have standards, which their programmers follow. However, each developer has his own idea about what is best. Standards have different metrics and theories. If there are excessive rules and standards, they can limit creativity and productivity. A design can be functional or internal design.

An internal design is good if the overall structure of the software code is clear, easily modifiable, understandable, and maintainable. It is robust with the capability to log status and with sufficient error handling. Furthermore, the software works as expected. A functional design is good if the software functionality comes from the requirements of the end user and customer. Even an inexperienced user can use the software without reading the user manual or seeking online help.

The software life cycle starts with the conception of the application and commences when the software is no longer used. It includes factors like requirements analysis, initial concept, internal design, functional design, test planning, documentation planning, document preparation, coding, maintenance, testing, integration, retesting, updates, and phase out.

A good software test engineer must possess a test to break attitude, which means that he must be able to focus on the detail in order to ensure that the application is of good quality. He must be diplomatic and tactful so that he can maintain a good relationship with the programmers, the customers, and the managements.

It is helpful if he has previous experience on software development so that he understands the whole process deeply. A good software test engineer is able to appreciate the point of view of the programmers. He must have good judgment skills to be able to determine critical or high-risk application areas that require testing.

A good quality assurance engineer also shares the same qualities with a good software test engineer. Furthermore, he must understand the whole process of software development and the organizations' goals and business approach. He must possess understanding of all sides of issues in order to communicate effectively with everyone concerned. He must be diplomatic and patient, especially in the early stages of the quality assurance process. Lastly, he must be able to detect problems during inspections and reviews.

Qualities Of A Good Quality Assurance Or Test Manager

A good manager must be familiar with the process of software development and must be enthusiastic and promote positivity in the team. He must be able to increase productivity by promoting teamwork and cooperation between quality assurance, software, and test engineers. If the processes require improvements, he must be diplomatic in ensuring smooth implementation of such changes.

He must be able to withstand pressure and offer the right feedback about quality issues to the other managers. He must be able to hire and keep the right personnel. He must possess strong communication skills to deal with everyone concerned in the process. Lastly, he must stay focused and be able to hold meetings.

Importance Of Documentation In Quality Assurance

If the team is large, it is more useful to have the proper documentation for efficient communication and management of projects. Documentation of quality assurance practices is necessary for repeatability. Designs, specifications, configurations, business rules, test plans, code changes, bug reports, test cases, and user manuals must have proper documentation. A system of documentation is necessary for easy obtaining and finding of information.

Each project has its own requirements. If it is an agile project, the requirements may change and evolve. Thus, there is no need for detailed documentation. However, it is useful to document user stories. Documentation on the software requirements describes the functionality and properties of the software. It must be clear, reasonably detailed, complete, attainable, cohesive, and testable. It may be difficult to organize and determine the details but there are tools and methods that are available.

It is important to exercise care in documenting the requirements of the project's customer, who may be an outside or in-house personnel, an end user, a customer contract officer, a customer acceptance tester, a customer manager, a sales person, or a software maintenance engineer. If the project did not meet the expectations, any of these customers can slow down the project.

Each organization has its own way of handling requirements. If the project is an agile project, the requirements are in the user stories. On the other hand, for other projects, the requirements are in the document. Some organizations may use functional specification and high-level project plans. In every requirement, documentation is important to help software testers to make test plans and perform testing. Without any significant documentation, it is impossible to determine if the application meets the user expectations.

Even if the requirements are not testable, it is still important to test the software. The test results must be oriented towards providing information about the risk levels and the status of the application. It is significant to have the correct testing approach to ensure success of the project. In an agile project, various approaches can use methods that require close cooperation and interaction among stakeholders.

Chapter 4: How To Develop And Run Software Testing

To develop the steps for software testing, it is necessary to consider the following.

First, it is important to get the requirements, user stories, internal design, functional design, and any other information that can help with the testing process.

Second, testing must have budget and schedule.

Third, it must have personnel with clear responsibilities.

Fourth, there must be project context to determine testing approaches, scope, and methods.

Fifth, identification of limitations and scope of tests is necessary in order to set priorities.

Sixth, testing must include methods and approaches applicable.

Seventh, it must have the requirements to determine the test environment.

Eighth, it must have requirements for testing tools.

Ninth, it is important to determine the data requirements for testing input.

Tenth, identification of labor requirements and tasks are important.

Eleventh, it must determine milestones, timelines, and schedule estimates.

Twelfth, testing must include error classes, boundary value analysis, and input equivalence classes, when needed.

Thirteenth, it must have a test plan and documents for approvals and reviews.

Fourteenth, testing must determine test scenarios and cases.

Fifteenth, it must include reviews, approvals of test cases, inspections, approaches, and scenarios.

Sixteenth, there must be testing tools and test environment, user manuals, configuration guides, reference documents, installation guides, test tracking processes, archiving and logging processes, and test input data.

Seventeenth, it must include software releases,

The Test Plan

A test plan is a document, which includes scope, objectives, and focus of the software testing activity. To prepare it, it is important to consider the efforts needed to validate the software's acceptability. The test plan must help even those people who are not part of the test group. Testing must be thorough but not very detailed.

The test plan can include the following: the title, the software version number, the plan's revision history, table of contents, the intended audience, the goal of testing, the overview of the software, relevant documents, legal or standards requirements, identifier and naming standards, and requirements for traceability. The test plan must also include overall project organization, test organization, dependencies and assumptions, risk analysis of the project, focus and priorities of testing, limitations and scope, test outline, data input outline, test environment, analysis of test environment validity, configuration and setup of test environment, and processes for software migration among other things.

A test case includes the input, event, or action plus its expected result in order to know if software's functionality is working as planned. It contains test case identifier, objective, test case name, test setup, requirements for input data, steps, and expected results. The details may differ, depending on the project context and organization. Some organizations handle test cases differently. Most of them use less-detailed test scenarios for simplicity and adaptability of test documentation. It is important to develop test cases because it is possible to detect problems and errors in the software through them.

When A Bug Is Discovered

If the software has a bug, the programmers must fix it. The software must undergo retesting after the resolution of the error. Regression testing must be able to check that the solutions performed were not able to create more problems within the application. A system for problem tracking must be set up so it becomes easier to perform the retesting. There are various software tools available to help the quality assurance team.

In tracking the problems, it is good to consider the following: complete information about the bug, bug identifier, present bug status, software version number, how the bug was discovered, specifics about environment and hardware, test case information, bug description, cause of the bug, fix description, retesting results, etc. There must be a reporting process so that the appropriate personnel will know about the errors and fixes.

A configuration management includes the various processes used to coordinate, control, and track requirements, code, problems, documentation, designs, change requests, tools, changes made, and person who made the changes. If the software has many bugs, the software tester must report them and focus on critical bugs. Because this problem can affect the schedule, the software tester must inform the managers and send documentation in order to substantiate the problem.

The decision to stop testing is difficult to do, especially for complex applications. In some cases, complete testing is not possible. Usually, the decision to stop testing considers the deadlines, the degree of test cases completion, the depletion of the test budget, the specified coverage of code, the reduction of the bug rate, and the ending of alpha or beta testing periods. If there is not enough time to perform thorough testing, it is important to focus the testing on important matters based on risk analysis. If the project is small, the testing can depend on risk analysis again.

In some cases, there are organizations that are not serious about quality assurance. For them, it is important to solve problems rather than prevent problems. Problems regarding software quality may not be evident. Furthermore, some organizations reward people who fix problems instead of incentivizing prevention of problems. Risk management includes actions that prevent things from happening. It is a shared responsibility among stakeholders. However, there must be a point person who is primarily responsible for it. In most cases, the responsibility falls on the quality assurance personnel.

Chapter 5: Deciding When To Release The Software To Users

In most projects, the decision to release the software depends on the timing of the end testing. However, for most applications, it is difficult to specify the release criteria without using subjectivity and assumptions. If the basis of the release criteria is the result of a specific test, there is an assumption that this test has addressed all the necessary software risks.

For many projects, this is impossible to do without incurring huge expenses. Therefore, the decision is actually a leap of faith. Furthermore, most projects try to balance cost, timeliness, and quality. As such, testing cannot address the balance of such factors when there is a need to decide on the release date.

Usually, the quality assurance or test manager decides when to release the software. However, this decision involves various assumptions. First, the test manager understands the considerations, which are significant in determining the quality of the software to justify release. Second, the quality of the software may not balance with cost and timeliness. In most organization, there is not enough definition for sufficient quality. Thus, it becomes very subjective and may vary from day to day or project to project.

The release criteria must consider the sales goals, deadlines, market considerations, legal requirements, quality norms of the business segment, programming and technical considerations, expectations of end users, internal budget, impact on the other projects, and a host of other factors. Usually, the project manager must know all these factors.

Because of the various considerations, it may not be possible for the quality assurance manager or test manager to decide the release of the software. However, he may be responsible in providing inputs to the project manager, who makes the release decision. If the project or the organization is small, the decision to release the software rests on the project manager or the product manager. For larger organizations or projects, there must be a committee to decide when to release the software.

If the software requirements change continuously, it is important for all stakeholders to cooperate from the beginning so that they all understand how the change in requirements may affect the project. They may decide on alternate strategies and test plans in advance. It is also beneficial to the project if the initial design of the software can accommodate changes later on. A well-documented code makes it easier for programmers to make the necessary changes.

It is also good to use rapid prototyping if possible so that customers will not make more requests for changes because they are sure of their requirements from the very beginning. The initial schedule of the project must allow extra lead-time for these changes. If possible, all changes must be in the "Phase 2" of the software version. It is important that only easily implemented requirements must be in the project.

The difficult ones must be in the future versions. The management and the customers must know about costs, inherent risks, and scheduling impacts of big changes in the requirements. If they know about the challenges, they can decide whether to continue with the changes or not.

There must be balance between expected efforts with the effort to set up automated testing for the changes. The design of the automated test scripts must be flexible. Its focus must be on aspects of application, which will remain unchanged. The reduction of the appropriate effort for the risk analysis of the changes can be through regression testing.

The design of the test cases must be flexible. The focus must be on ad-hoc testing and not on detailed test cases and test plans. If there is a continuous request for changes in the requirements, it is unreasonable to expect that requirements will remain stable and pre-determined. Thus, it may be appropriate to use approaches for agile development.

It is difficult to determine if software has significant hidden or unexpected functionality. It also indicates that the software development process has deeper problems. The functionality must be removed if does not serve any purpose to the software because it may have unknown dependencies or impacts. If not removed, there must be a consideration for the determination of regression testing needs and risks. The management must know if there are significant risks caused by the unexpected functionality.

The implementation of quality assurance processes is slow over time because the stakeholders must have a consensus. There must be an alignment of processes and organizational goals. As the organization matures, there will be an improvement on productivity. Problem prevention will be the focus. There will be a reduction of burnout and panics. There will be less wasted effort and more improved focus.

The processes must be efficient and simple to prevent any "Process Police" mentality. Furthermore, quality assurance processes promote automated reporting and tracking thereby minimizing paperwork. However, in the short run, implementation may be slow. There will be more days for inspections, reviews, and planning but less time for handling angry end users and late night fixing of errors.

If the growth of the IT organization is very rapid, fixed quality assurance processes may be impossible. Thus, it is important to hire experienced people. The management must prioritize issues about quality and maintain a good relationship with the customers. Every employee must know what quality means to the end user.

Chapter 6: Using Automated Testing Tools

If the project is small, learning and implementing the automated testing tools may not be worth it. However, these automated testing tools are important for large projects. These tools use a standard coding language like Java, ruby, python, or other proprietary scripting language. In some cases, it is necessary to record the first tests for the generation of the test scripts. Automated testing is challenging if there are continuous changes to the software because a change in test code is necessary every time there is a new requirement. In addition, the analysis and interpretation of results can be difficult.

Data driven or keyword driven testing is common in functional testing. The maintenance of actions and data is easy through a spreadsheet. The test drivers read the information for them to perform the required tests. This strategy provides more control, documentation, development, and maintenance of test cases. Automated tools can include code analyzers, coverage analyzers, memory analyzers, load/performance test tools, web test tools, and other tools.

A test engineer, who does manual testing, determines if the application performs as expected. He must be able to judge the expected outcome. However, in an automated test, the computer judges the test outcome. A mechanism must be present for the computer to compare automatically between the actual and expected outcomes for every test scenario. If the test engineer is new to automated testing, it is important that he undergo training first.

Proper planning and analysis are important in selecting and using an automated tool for testing. The right tool must be able to test more thoroughly than manual methods. It must test faster and allow continuous integration. It must also reduce the tedious manual testing. The automation of testing is costly. However, it may be able to provide savings in the long term.

Choosing The Appropriate Test Environment

There is always a tradeoff between cost and test environment. The ultimate scenario is to have a collection of test environments, which mirror exactly all possible usage, data, network, software, and hardware characteristics that the software can use. For most software, it is impossible to predict all environment variations. Furthermore, for complex and large systems, it is extremely expensive to duplicate a live environment.

The reality is that decisions on the software environment characteristics are important. Furthermore, the choice of test environments takes into consideration logistical, budget, and time constraints. People with the most technical experience and knowledge, as well as with the deep understanding of constraints and risks, make these decisions. If the project is low risk or small, it is common to take the informal approach. However, for high risk or large projects, it is important to take a more formalize procedure with many personnel.

It is also possible to coordinate internal testing with efforts for beta testing. In addition, it is possible to create built-in automated tests upon software installation by users. The tests are able to report information through the internet about problems and application environment encountered. Lastly, it is possible to use virtual environments.

The Best Approach To Test Estimation

It is not easy to find the best approach because it depends on the IT organization, the project, as well as the experience of the people involved. If there are two projects with the same size and complexity, the right test effort for life-critical medical software may be very large compared to a project involving an inexpensive computer game. The choice of a test estimation approach based on complexity and size may be applicable to a project but not to the other one.

The implicit risk context approach caters to a quality assurance manager or project manager, who uses risk context with past personal experiences to allocate resources for testing. The risk context assumes that each project is similar to the others. It is an experience-based intuitive guess.

The metrics-based approach, on the other hand, uses past experiences on different projects. If there is already data from a number of projects, the information is beneficial in future test planning. For each new project, the basis of adjustment of required test time is the available metrics. In essence, this is not easy to do because it is judgment based on historical experience.

The test-work breakdown approach decomposes the testing tasks into smaller tasks to estimate testing with a reasonable accuracy. It assumes that the breakdown of testing tasks is predictable and accurate and that it is feasible to estimate the testing effort. If the project is large, this is not feasible because there is a need to extend testing time if there are many bugs. In addition to, there is a need to extend development time.

The iterative approach is for large test projects. An initial rough estimate is necessary prior to testing. Once testing begins and after finishing a small percentage of testing work, there is a need to update the testing estimate because testers have already obtained additional knowledge of the issues, risks, and software quality. There is also a need to update test schedules and plans. After finishing a larger percentage of testing work, the testing estimate requires another update. The cycle continues until testing ends.

The percentage-of-development approach requires a quick way of testing estimation. If the project has 1,000 hours of estimated programming effort, the

IT firm usually assigns a 40% ratio for testing. Therefore, it will allot 400 hours for testing. The usefulness of this approach depends on risk, software type, personnel, and complexity level.

In an agile software development approach, the test estimate is unnecessary if the project uses pure test-driven development although it is common to mix some automated unit tests with either automated or manual functional testing. By the nature of agile-based projects, they are not dependent on testing efforts but on the construction of the software.

Conclusion

Thank you again for purchasing this book!

I hope this book was able to help you to understand the concepts of Software Quality Assurance.

The next step is to apply what you learned from this book to your work.

Finally, if you enjoyed this book, please take the time to share your thoughts and post a review on Amazon. It'd be greatly appreciated!

Thank you and good luck!

www.ingramcontent.com/pod-product-compliance
Lightning Source LLC
Chambersburg PA
CBHW060931050326
40689CB00013B/3047
9781523866670